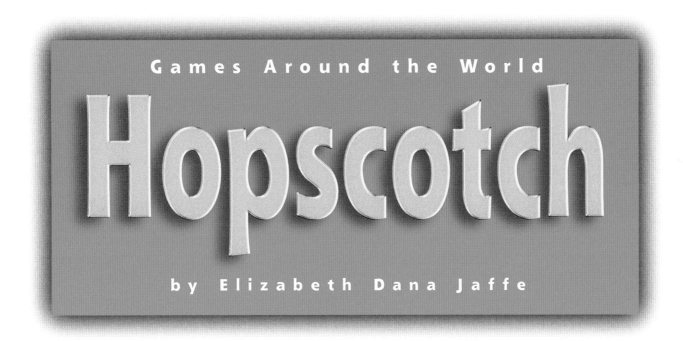

Games Around the World

Hopscotch

by Elizabeth Dana Jaffe

Content Adviser: Professor Sherry L. Field, Department of Social Science Education, College of Education, The University of Georgia

Reading Adviser: Dr. Linda D. Labbo, Department of Reading Education, College of Education, The University of Georgia

COMPASS POINT BOOKS

MINNEAPOLIS, MINNESOTA

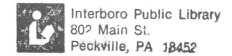

Compass Point Books
3722 West 50th Street, #115
Minneapolis, MN 55410

Visit Compass Point Books on the Internet at *www.compasspointbooks.com* or e-mail your request to
custserv@compasspointbooks.com

Photographs ©: Gregg Andersen, cover, 5; Jeremy Horner/Corbis, 4; Richard T. Nowitz/Corbis, 6; N. Carter/North
Wind Picture Archives, 8; Bettmann/Corbis, 10; Unicorn Stock Photos/Angela Blume, 13; International Stock/Geroge
Ancona, 14; TRIP/S. Grant, 15; Photo Network/Bill Bachmann, 26; TRIP/J. Stanley, 27.

Editors: E. Russell Primm and Emily J. Dolbear
Photo Researcher: Svetlana Zhurkina
Photo Selector: Linda S. Koutris
Designer: Bradfordesign, Inc.
Illustrator: Abby Bradford

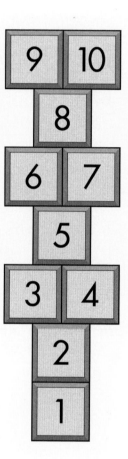

Library of Congress Cataloging-in-Publication Data

Jaffe, Elizabeth D.
    Hopscotch / by Elizabeth Dana Jaffe ; content adviser, Sherry L. Field ; reading adviser, Linda D.
Labbo.
        p. cm. — (Games around the world)
    Includes bibliographical references and index.
    ISBN 0-7565-0133-4 (hardcover : lib. bdg.)
        1. Hopscotch—Juvenile literature. [1. Hopscotch.] I. Field, Sherry L. II. Labbo, Linda D. III. Title.
GV1218.H6 J34 2002
796.2—dc21
                                                                                    2001001584

Table of Contents

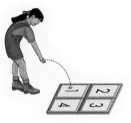

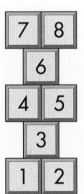

Toss, Hop, Jump

First you toss a tiny stone in a square. Then you hop from one square to the next. Hop on one foot. Jump on two feet. Hop on one foot. Jump on two. Keep going. Pick up the tiny stone. Now hop back to the first square again. You are playing hopscotch!

You don't need many things to play this game. You need a small object to toss, a sidewalk or playground, and some chalk. You can also play on soft ground, but then, you'll need a stick to make your hopscotch **pattern**.

As you'll see, it is a fun and easy game. That's why children around the world play hopscotch.

▲ *A hopscotch pattern in chalk*

◀ *Three children play hopscotch in India.*

5

The History of Hopscotch

People have played the game of hopscotch for many hundreds of years. The Romans might have played hopscotch first. They cut a hopscotch pattern into the floor of a forum. (A forum is the town square of an old Roman city.) The early hopscotch patterns were round. These patterns looked like wheels.

Long ago, ancient Rome ruled most of the world. The Romans took over many countries, including Britain. They brought their way of life to these countries.

Why Is It Called Hopscotch?

Hopscotch is an English name. When you play hopscotch, you hop over the "scotch." The scotch is the line on the ground the players hop over. (The small object you throw in a hopscotch game is sometimes called a scotch too.)

◀ *An old Roman hopscotch pattern is in the shape of a wheel.*

In Britain, Roman soldiers played hopscotch on the Great North Road. This long road went from Glasgow, Scotland, to London, England. Some of the hopscotch courts the Romans made were more than 100 feet (31 meters) long!

The Roman soldiers often played hopscotch to test their strength and speed. Carrying heavy weights, they hopped through the courts as fast as they could. They liked playing this game.

The Romans shared the game with the British children they met. The children enjoyed it too. They played it with their friends and family. Hopscotch soon spread across Britain. And it was passed down through the years.

Then in the 1600s, many people left Scotland and England. They moved to what would become the United States of America and settled there. They hoped to begin a new life.

◀ *Roman soldiers played hopscotch on the Great North Road.*

These settlers brought their beliefs, ways of life, and games to the Americas. Among the games they brought was hopscotch! The children of early American colonists played hopscotch.

Roman soldiers took over other countries in Europe. They brought hopscotch with them. Over time, hopscotch has become a favorite children's game around the world. Children from Alaska to Asia play hopscotch!

◀ *Girls play a hopscotch game in the Netherlands in the 1950s.*

How to Play Hopscotch

In all hopscotch games, players hop through a pattern on the ground in a certain way. In some games, players throw or kick a small object called a **marker** through the pattern. The spaces between the lines are called the **squares**.

You can use almost anything as a marker. A small stick, a stone, a button, a bunch of keys, or a coin will work well.

Children in other parts of the world use shells, beanbags, or fruit pits. They sometimes use pieces of glass! Choose your marker carefully. It must be easy to throw or kick through the pattern.

> ## What Else Do You Call Markers and Squares?
>
> A marker is also called a puck, a stone, a potsy, or a scotch. Squares are also called boxes, dens, beds, steps, houses, or nests.

This hopscotch player is using a stone for a marker. ▶

Rules for hopscotch games are different around the world. Over time, players have changed the rules of the game to suit their needs. One rule is the same wherever you play hopscotch—you can never touch the lines.

▲ *Drawing hopscotch squares on the playground*

Hopscotch Don'ts!

- Don't throw the marker in the wrong square or on a line.
- Don't lose your balance.
- Don't step on a line or in the square the marker is in.
- Don't put both feet in one square.

◀ *Remember, you can't touch the lines!*

Potsy—A Game from the United States

Children first played potsy in New York City. They drew the pattern with chalk on the sidewalks and streets.

Number of players:	Two or more
What you need:	Chalk and a marker (a stone, a bottle cap, an eraser, or anything else that will not roll away)
Setup:	Draw a pattern with eight squares and number them from 1 to 8
Object:	To complete the whole pattern after everyone has had a turn

How to play:

1. Players take turns—one at a time.

2. The first player throws a marker into square 1.

3. The player hops on one foot into square 2 and then into square 3.

4. The player hops and lands with one foot in square 4 and the other foot in square 5. The player then hops into square 6. The player hops again and lands with one foot in square 7 and the other foot in square 8.

5. Here, the player jumps and turns around. The player must land with one foot in square 7 and the other foot in square 8.

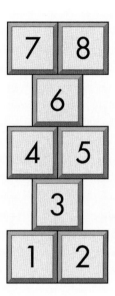

▲ *A potsy pattern*

Why Is It Called Potsy?

Players called the marker a "potsy." That's how this game got its name.

▲ Hopping back to square 2

6. The player hops all the way back, following the pattern to square 2.

7. In square 2, standing on one leg, the player must bend over and pick up the marker in square 1.

8. The player then hops into square 1 and then hops out of the pattern.

9. The player who completes this pattern goes on to throw the marker into square 2 and goes through the pattern in order. The player must always hop over the square with the marker in it, and pick it up on the way back.

10. A player who completes the whole pattern with no mistakes can put his or

18

her **initials** in any square. The initialed square is then a resting place for this player. The other players must hop over it.

11. A player who makes a mistake loses his or her turn.

12. The winner is the first player to complete the pattern after everyone has had a turn.

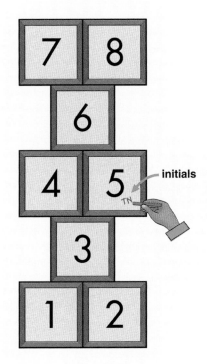

▲ After you complete the pattern, you can put your initials in any square.

Escargot—A Game from France

Children in France play escargot on a sidewalk or a playground. They draw the pattern in chalk. Sometimes, schoolyards have escargot patterns painted on them. No marker is used in escargot.

Number of players:	Two or more
What you need:	Chalk
Setup:	Draw a snail's shell with squares big enough to hop in. The pattern can have as many squares as you like. Number the squares starting with number 1.
Object:	To win the greatest number of **houses**
How to play:	
1.	The first player hops through the pattern toward the

center of the spiral. The player must hop into every square on the same foot and not step on any lines.

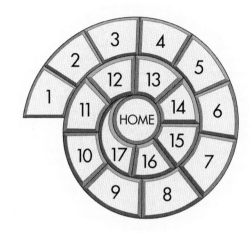

▲ *A large escargot pattern*

2. At the center square of the snail's shell, the player can rest with both feet on the ground.

3. Then the player turns around to follow the pattern back.

4. A player who hops through the pattern without any mistakes can go again. If the player makes any mistakes, the next player gets a turn.

5. A player who has hopped through the pattern twice may pick a house. That means the player can write his or her

Why Is It Called Escargot?

Escargot means "snail" in French. The pattern in this game is shaped like a snail's shell.

21

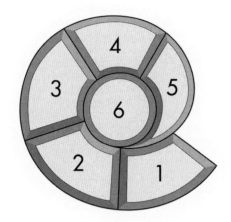

▲ *A small escargot pattern*

▲ *As the squares fill up with initials, the game gets harder!*

initials in any square. This house is a resting place for only this player. All other players must hop over it.

6. As the game continues, many or all of the squares become houses for different players. The houses make it difficult for the players to hop to the center square of the snail's shell. When there are too many houses to continue playing, the game is over.

7. The winner is the player who has the most houses at the end of the game.

Chilly—A Game from India

In India, children play chilly in the soft, red soil. They draw a hopscotch pattern on the ground with a stick or a stone. They don't write in the squares. The marker is kicked through the pattern.

Number of players: Two or more

What you need: A stick or stone and a marker (a flat stone works well)

Setup: Draw a pattern with four or six squares

Object: To complete the pattern first after everyone has had a turn

How to play:

1. The first player stands in front of the pattern. He or she throws the marker into the nearest square on the left side of the pattern.

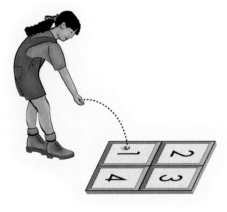

▲ *Throw your marker into the first square.*

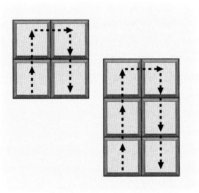

▲ *You hop in the same direction in four and six square patterns.*

2. If the marker lands in the correct square, the player hops into this square on one foot.

3. Then, with the hopping foot, he or she kicks the marker into the next square. The player continues through the pattern in this way.

4. When the player completes the pattern, he or she kicks the marker out of the pattern. Then, the player goes again.

5. The player picks up his or her marker. He or she throws it into the second square on the left side of the pattern.

6. If the marker lands in the correct square, the player hops over the first square of the pattern into the second square.

7. The player then hops and kicks the marker through the rest of the pattern.

8. A player who makes a mistake loses his or her turn. The player's next turn starts where this one stopped.

9. The winner is the player who completes the pattern first after everyone has had a turn.

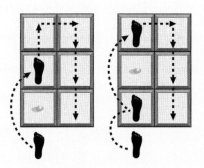

▲ *Always hop over the square with the marker in it.*

Why Is It Called Chilly?

We don't know! We can only guess how this game got its name. Do you have any ideas?

Playing Your Own Hopscotch Game

Now you know how children play hopscotch around the world. Of course, many other kinds of hopscotch games are played in many other countries. The differences between the games make them interesting.

Learn as many hop-scotch games as you can. Think up different rules with your friends. You can make up your own hopscotch games. A place to play, a piece of chalk, and a small stone for a marker are all you need!

▲ *An escargot pattern is painted on the schoolyard.*

◀ *Playing hopscotch can be lots of fun.*

Glossary

initials—the first letter of your first name and the first letter of your last name

houses—squares that one player may rest in and all the other players must hop over

marker—the object a player throws or kicks through a hopscotch pattern

pattern—the form shaped by squares that hopscotch players hop through

squares—the shapes that form the pattern

Did You Know?

1. Girls in New York City used to play potsy using bobby pins as markers.

2. Hopscotch is called *marelle* in France, *hinkelbaan* in the Netherlands, *pico* in Vietnam, *rayuela* in Argentina, and *ekaria dukaria* in India.

3. At the beach, you can play hopscotch in the sand.

4. You can play hopscotch as a board game.

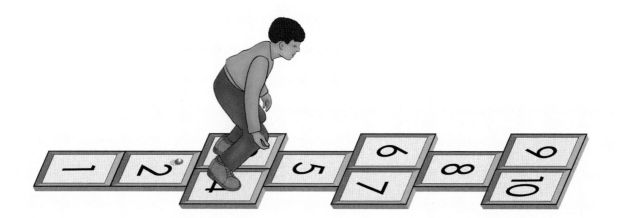

Want to Know More?

At the Library

Erlbach, Arlene. *Sidewalk Games Around the World*. Brookfield, Conn.: Millbrook Press, 1997.

Gryski, Camilla. *Let's Play: Traditional Games of Childhood*. Buffalo, N.Y.: Kids Can Press, 1998.

Lankford, Mary D. *Hopscotch: Around the World, Nineteen Ways to Play the Game*. New York: Beech Tree, 1992.

Maguire, Jack. *Hopscotch, Hangman, Hot Potato, and Ha, Ha, Ha*. New York: Simon and Schuster, 1990.

On the Web

Children's Games from Around the World—Hopscotch

http://www.rice.edu/projects/topics/edition11/games-hopscotch.htm

For instructions on how to play two hopscotch games

Hopscotch

http://www.gameskidsplay.net/games/other_games/hopscotch.htm

For the basic rules of hopscotch

Through the Mail

The Children's Museum

Museum Kits Program

300 Congress Street

Boston, MA 02210-1034

To order a museum kit about multicultural hopscotch games

On the Road

Canadian Children's Museum

at the Canadian Museum of Civilization

100 Laurier Street

Hull, Quebec J8X 4H2

Canada

819/776-8294

To visit an exhibit with old and new toys and games from around the world

Index

About the Author
After graduating from Brown University, Elizabeth Dana Jaffe received her master's degree in early education from Bank Street College of Education. Since then, she has written and edited educational materials. Elizabeth Dana Jaffe lives in New York City.